DISCOVER AND DO

GEOGRAPHY

CARING FOR OUR EARTH

Enslow
PUBLISHING

Published in 2024 by Enslow Publishing, LLC
2544 Clinton Street
Buffalo, NY 14224

Copyright © 2021 Franklin Watts, a division of Hachette Children's Group

Editor: Katie Dicker
Designer: Clare Nicholas
Series designer: Rocket Design (East Anglia) Ltd

Manufactured in the United States of America

CPSIA compliance information: Batch #CSENS24: For further information contact
Enslow Publishing LLC, New York, New York at 1-800-398-2504.

Please visit our website, www.enslowpublishing.com. For a free color catalog of all our high-quality books,
call toll free 1-800-398-2504 or fax 1-877-980-4454.

Cataloging-in-Publication Data

Names: Lacey, Jane.
Title: Caring for our earth / Jane Lacey.
Description: New York : Enslow, 2024. | Series: Discover and do: geography |
Includes glossary, index and bibliographic information.
Identifiers: ISBN 9781978534643 (pbk) | ISBN 9781978534650 (library bound) | ISBN 9781978534667 (ebook)
Subjects: LCSH: Conservation of natural resources-- Juvenile literature | Earth (planet)--Juvenile literature |
Environmental protection--Juvenile literature | Natural resources--Juvenile literature
Classification: LCC TD170.15 L33 2024 | DDC 333.7--dc23

Picture credits:
t=top b=bottom m=middle l=left r=right

Shutterstock: krissikunterbunt cover/title page l, Amanita Silvicora 4 and 24b, Val_Iva 5tl and 10b, StockAppeal 5tr and
8t, natianis 5br and 10t, idorie 6–7, Natty_Blissful 7t and 31b, Designer things 7b, naulicrea 9t, ByEmo 12t, Macrovector
13t, toyotoyo 13mr and 29b, elenabsl 14t, Pogorelova Olga 14b and 30t, N.Savranska 15t, what is my name 15bm,
Meilun 15b, Banana Walking 16t, pandora64 16b, DeawSS 18t, Merggy 18m, Seahorse Vector 18b and 28, Marina
Akinina 19t, MichaelJayBerlin 19ml, Konstantin Remizov 19mr, Noam Armonn 19br, NotionPic 20t and 29t, MuchMania
20b, piscary 21t, VVadyab Pico 22t and 31m, Rhoeo 22b, SurfsUp 23t, taviphoto 23mr, Lalam photography 23bl, Zvereva
Yana 24t, Natali Snailcat 25t, I love photo 25bm, Don Mammoser 25br, Neungstockr 26t, Auspicious 26b and 31t; Getty:
VasjaKoman cover/title page r, Jiraporn Meereewee 8b, Wavebreakmedia 9mr and 32, shulz 9bl, SurfUpVector 12b and
30b, Rumi Fujishima 17t.

All design elements from Shutterstock.
Craft models from a previous series by Q2AMedia.

Find us on

DISCOVER AND DO

GEOGRAPHY

CARING FOR OUR EARTH

Written by Jane Lacey

Enslow
PUBLISHING

CONTENTS

Words that appear in **bold** can be found in the glossary on pages 28–29.

PLANET EARTH

Earth, the planet we live on, is amazing. Animals and plants live almost everywhere. Hills and valleys are covered in flowers, deep seas are full of fish, and people live in big cities and tiny villages.

Careful living

Some of the things we do in our daily lives can harm the planet and the plants and animals that live here. However, there are many other things we can do to take care of planet Earth.

Earth is the only planet we know of that has air and water and is the right temperature to support life.

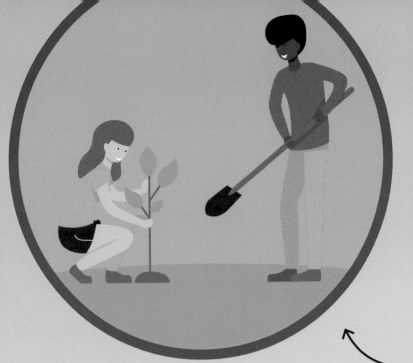

Air

All living things need air to survive. Animals, including people, breathe in **oxygen**, a gas in the air, and breathe out the gas **carbon dioxide**. Plants take in carbon dioxide and give off oxygen.

Trees help keep the air full of oxygen for us to breathe. We should plant trees to replace those we use.

Global warming

Earth is kept warm by a layer of gases that traps heat from the sun. When **fossil fuels** are burned, they release a lot of carbon dioxide into the air. This traps even more heat from the sun. We call this "**global warming**."

This power station burns fossil fuels to generate electricity. The burning fuels release gases that can harm the planet.

WATER

All life on Earth depends on water. About three-quarters of the planet is covered in water, but most of this is salty sea water we can't drink. Only a small amount is fresh water.

Most of Earth's water can be found in the oceans.

Water all around us

The water on Earth goes around and around in a cycle. It falls on land and sea as rain, sleet, or snow. When the sun warms this water, it **evaporates** and rises into the air to forms clouds. The water falls to Earth again as rain and collects in lakes, rivers, and streams.

cloud

rain

Water constantly moves in the water cycle.

evaporation

Precious water

In hot countries, there is very little water. Water is precious in wet countries, too, because cleaning water costs money and uses **energy**. We can care for the planet by not wasting clean water that pours from our taps. We should only take the water that we need.

Water is cleaned at a water treatment plant.

ACTIVITY

SAVE WATER WHEN YOU BRUSH!

❶ Put a bowl or pitcher in the sink. Leave the tap running while you brush your teeth for 1 minute.

❷ Use a measuring cup to figure out how much water came out of the tap during the minute you let it run.

❸ Use this water to wash your hands, water plants, or fill a birdbath.

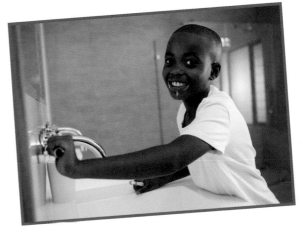

How many people live in your home? If they turn off the tap every time they brush their teeth, how much clean water will your household save?

WHERE I LIVE

Do you live in a big city or a tiny village? Wherever you live, you can make your area a better place for the people, plants, and animals that live there.

Welcoming wildlife

If you have a garden or window box, you can plant flowers to attract bees and butterflies. An area full of plant life encourages birds, small animals, and insects to visit. A tree helps keep the air clean.

If you do not have a garden, you can still use a window box or potted plant.

Colorful wildflowers are popular with bees and butterflies.

HOW COULD YOUR AREA BE IMPROVED?

1 Draw a plan of the area around your home (A). Include features such as buildings, roads, parks, crosswalks, and parking lots.

2 Ask the following questions:
   a) Is it a good place for people, plants, and animals to live?
   b) Is it clean and safe?
   c) How could it be improved?

3 Now draw the plan again, adding features that you think would improve the area (B).

KEY
- buildings
- grass
- road
- cars
- lake

KEY
- trees
- crosswalk
- pathway
- playground
- parking lot

TRAVELING AROUND

The way we choose to travel around affects the planet. Cars, buses, and trucks burn fossil fuels that pollute the air with carbon emissions.

Short journeys

For short journeys, it is easy to walk or bike. These forms of exercise help keep us fit. Walking and biking are good for the planet, too, because they don't use fossil fuels. They are useful ways to travel around without causing **pollution**.

When fossil fuels power a car's engine, exhaust fumes (carbon emissions) are released.

If you walk or bike to school, you use your own energy to move.

Long journeys

For longer journeys we need to use cars, buses, trains, or planes. Using public transportation and carpooling help reduce the number of vehicles that are used. This cuts pollution and carbon emissions.

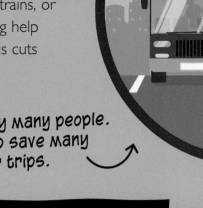

Buses carry many people. They help save many car trips.

ACTIVITY

CHOOSE THE BEST JOURNEY

❶ Find out the distance between your home and your school.

❷ How long does the journey take:
   a) by foot?
   b) by bike?
   c) by bus?
   d) by car?

❸ Which journeys are good for your health? Why do you think this is?

❹ Which journeys are bad for the planet? How could they be improved?

Collect information about your journey to school and create a chart like the one shown below.

Transportation	Time	Good for planet?	Good for me?	Comments
walk	25 minutes	5 stars	5 stars	fun in good weather
bike	12 minutes	5 stars	5 stars	bike lanes essential
bus	10 minutes	3 stars	2 stars	have to walk from the bus stop
car	5 minutes	1 star	1 star	nowhere to park but very quick!

LITTER

Litter is any garbage that hasn't been thrown away or recycled. Litter is dirty and can be dangerous to wildlife.

The effects of litter

Some animals mistake litter for food. They can choke on it or be poisoned. Other animals get trapped in litter. Broken glass may cut them. Litter in the street gets washed down drains, where it flows into rivers and the sea. It can pollute the water, block pipes, and cause flooding.

Our garbage is a danger to ocean creatures.

The pollution in this river is a threat to plant and animal life.

Litter at school

Children who keep their school playground free of litter set a good example to others. Garbage bins, recycling programs, litter pickups, and poster campaigns can all help make a difference.

You can help to keep parks and playgrounds clean.

DESIGN AN ANTI-LITTER POSTER

Think of a poster that would make everyone at your school stop and think before leaving litter behind.

1 What message do you want to get across? What are the most important points?

2 What words and pictures will help you get your message across clearly?

3 Use strong, bright colors and short, catchy phrases.

Trash Hurts the Planet!

Please Recycle!

REDUCE, REUSE!

The things we use are made of materials. Our socks are often made of cotton, for example. The paper in this book comes from wood, and the pens we write with are made of plastic.

Oil is used to make plastic products. We use oil for fuel too, but it is running out.

Renewable and non-renewable

Some materials are **renewable**. Cotton and wood, for example, can be grown and replaced. Other materials, such as metal and plastic (which is made from oil), are **non-renewable**. One day these materials will run out.

Cotton is a renewable material because it can be grown again and again.

Think before you throw!

We throw away all kinds of things that could be used again. Making the most of materials is a good way of saving the planet's resources. If you no longer want something, you could always give it to someone else to use.

You could mend, embroider, or decorate your clothes to give them new life instead of throwing them away.

ACTIVITY

REUSE PAPER TO MAKE A NOTEPAD

You will need:
- **small cardboard box**
- **colorful paper, stickers, or paint**
- **glue**
- **string**
- **pen or pencil**
- **scissors**
- **hole punch**
- **half-used paper**

1 If your box has a lid, cut it off. Cut off part of one of the sides as well and decorate the box.

4 Punch a hole in the side of the box. Tie a pencil or pen to a piece of string and attach the string to the box.

Put your pad in your room for reminder notes or in the kitchen for shopping lists. Keep it full of used paper. When the paper can't be used anymore, recycle it.

2 Take the half-used paper and cut each sheet into pieces small enough to fit in the box.

3 Place the cut paper in the box, clean side up.

RECYCLE!

If you can't reuse something, you may be able to recycle it instead of throwing it away. Recycling means using the materials that objects are made from to make something new.

The garbage we throw away is burned or buried in the ground.

Running out of room

Garbage has to go somewhere. It is usually recycled, burned, or buried in a **landfill site**. Burying our garbage keeps it out of sight while it **rots**, but we are running out of places to put it. Today we can recycle many materials, including paper, plastic, metal, and glass.

GLASS

ORGANIC

PLASTIC

Recycling helps to cut down on garbage and saves the energy used to make new materials.

Organic and inorganic

Organic materials come from things that were once alive. Examples include food (from plants and animals) and paper (from wood). **Inorganic** materials, such as glass, metal, and plastic, have never been alive.

Organic materials rot and decay. They can be turned into compost and dug back into the soil.

FIND OUT HOW GARBAGE DECAYS

You will need:
- **two buckets**
- **soil and leaves**
- **two cloths**

1 Collect garbage from school lunches. Sort it into:
 a) organic materials (such as apple cores, banana peels, crusts of bread)
 b) inorganic materials (such as plastic containers, food wrappers, glass bottles)

2 Bury the inorganic garbage in one bucket of soil and leaves. Bury the organic garbage in another bucket of soil and leaves.

3 Water both buckets lightly and cover them with a cloth.

4 After about eight weeks, you should find that the organic material has rotted into the soil and the inorganic material is still sitting in the soil.

POLLUTION

Pollution is harmful matter that gets into the air, soil, and water. We can help care for the planet by keeping the environment free of pollution.

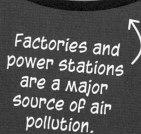

Smog

In big cities on sunny days, the exhaust fumes from vehicles can combine with the air to form **smog**. Smog is a mixture of smoke and fog. It is like a thick, dirty cloud. Using public transport to cut exhaust fumes from cars is one way to reduce smog levels.

Factories and power stations are a major source of air pollution.

Vehicle fumes can get trapped in the air in a busy city.

Dirty water

When streams and rivers become polluted with litter, it can harm plants and wildlife and make our drinking water dirty. Chemical and oil spills at sea spread very quickly and have a devastating effect on local wildlife.

When oil is transported around the world, there is risk of an oil leak or tanker disaster.

ACTIVITY

MONITOR AIR POLLUTION

You will need:
- **scissors**
- **five large squares of light-colored cloth**
- **five small squares of dark-colored cloth**
- **glue stick**

1 Cut one of the small pieces of cloth into a leaf shape.

2 Lightly glue your leaf-shaped cloth to the middle of a large piece of cloth.

3 Hang the two pieces of cloth outside, by a window or a place sheltered from rain.

4 After about a week, pull the pieces of cloth apart. You should find that the small cloth has left a leaf shape in the middle of the large cloth. Pollution in the air will have made the exposed cloth dirty.

5 Try the activity a few more times with new pieces of cloth, hanging the cloths in different places to see which areas are most polluted.

LOCAL WILDLIFE

Wherever we live, we share our local area with other animals. Farms, buildings, and roads change the environment. They make it difficult for wildlife to find food and shelter.

City life

We can care for the planet by helping to make our local area a good place for wildlife as well as people. Cities are built for people to live and work in, but they are home to plants and animals, too.

Our roads and urban spaces change the habitat of local wildlife.

A city park is a space that can be shared by people and local wildlife.

Countryside

In the countryside, there is plenty of green space, but animals can still be threatened. Fields of crops are sprayed with poisonous **pesticides**. On some farms, fences and cages prevent animals from roaming freely and finding food.

Good farming practices allow chickens, ducks, and geese to move around.

MAKE A BIRD STATION

Help encourage local wildlife with a bird station.

You will need:
- **bird feeder**
- **bird food**
- **bowl of water**
- **paper**
- **pen or pencil**

1 Hang a bird feeder on a branch or pole.

2 Put out a bowl of water nearby for the birds to drink from and wash in.

3 Keep a record of the birds that visit your bird station.

sparrow — ||||| ||||| |||||
blue jay — ||||| ||||| |||||
||||| |||||

HABITATS

Deserts, mountains, rain forests, and the seashore are all **habitats**. They are home to particular plants and animals. We need to look after these habitats to make sure that all the plants and creatures survive.

Desert creatures can handle hot, dry conditions.

Changing habitats

Global warming is changing some habitats and putting the plants and animals that live there at risk. As planet Earth warms, rivers dry up, plants die, and animals have no water to drink.

As Earth gets warmer, icebergs melt and polar animals lose their habitat.

Coral reefs

Coral reefs take a long time to grow. They are home to many ocean plants and animals. They shelter coastal waters and protect the mainland from storm waves.

Global warming makes the sea too warm for coral reefs to survive. This puts other plants and animals at risk.

ACTIVITY

ADOPT AN ANIMAL

1 Ask an adult to help you use the internet to research how to adopt an animal. Orangutans, for example, are endangered because the forests they live in are being cut down. The money you give can help to save the forests and the orangutans.

2 Think of how you can raise some money for your adopted animal. You could hold a garage sale to get rid of unwanted things at the same time.

3 Find some pictures of your adopted animal in magazines or using the internet. Display them to advertise your cause!

ENERGY

Energy is the power that makes things work. At home, we use a type of energy called electricity to work our lights, televisions, washing machines, and fridges.

Saving energy

We burn fossil fuels to release energy. We need to use this energy carefully because fossil fuels are running out. We also need to reduce the carbon emissions they produce. At home, we can turn off lights and turn down the heating to save energy. In the future, we need to find energy sources that will not run out. The sun, the wind, and water are all types of renewable energy that cause less pollution.

We use electric lights at home to light up the dark.

Strong sea breezes turn the blades of these wind turbines to generate electricity.

MAKE A WINDSOCK

You will need:

- 12 x 3 inch (30 x 8 cm) strip of construction paper
- plastic bag cut into a 12 x 12-inch (30 x 30 cm) square
- stapler
- hole puncher
- string
- paper clip
- garden stake, about 5 feet (1.5 m) tall
- tape

1 Punch three holes 4 inches (10 cm) apart along the long edge of the paper.

2 Cut the plastic square into strips, leaving an uncut strip at the top. Staple to the long card edge without the holes.

3 Connect the ends of the paper together to make a cylinder and staple securely.

4 Tie three pieces of string, 8 inches (20 cm) long, to the three holes and tie these to a paper clip.

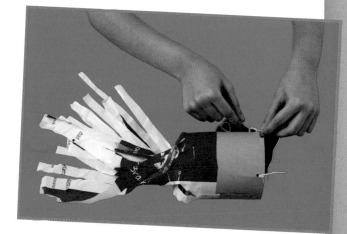

5 Tie the paper clip to a piece of string 24 inches (60 cm) long and tape this to the top of a garden stake. Fix the stake in the ground.

You can tell the strength of the wind by the height of your windsock. What might be good about wind power? What might be bad?

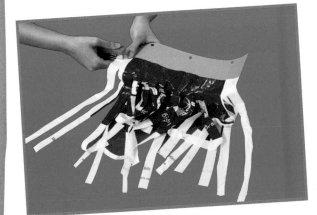

Glossary

carbon dioxide

Carbon dioxide is a gas in the air. People and animals breathe out carbon dioxide, while plants absorb it.

carbon emissions

Carbon emissions are gases containing carbon that are sent into the air when we burn fossil fuels such as coal, oil, and gas.

coral reef

A coral reef is a ridge of living coral growing on top of coral skeletons. A coral reef lies just below the water in warm seas.

electricity

Electricity is a kind of energy. We use electricity in our homes and schools to give us light and to work machines.

energy

Energy is the force that makes things move, heat up, or change.

environment

The environment is the surroundings in which people, plants, and animals live.

evaporates

Water evaporates when it heats up and changes from a liquid into a gas called water vapor. This change is called evaporation.

fossil fuel

A fossil fuel is a type of fuel that contains carbon. Fossil fuels release carbon into the air when they are burned.

global warming

Global warming is the rise in Earth's temperature. It is partly caused by a buildup of gases in the air when we burn fossil fuels.

habitat

A habitat is the natural surrounding that is home to an animal or a plant. For example, the desert is the habitat of a cactus plant.

inorganic

Inorganic materials are materials that have never been alive. Metal and glass are inorganic materials.

landfill site

A landfill site is a huge pit in the ground where garbage is buried.

materials

Materials are the different substances that are used to make the things around us.

non-renewable

Non-renewable energy or materials cannot be replaced. When they are used up, they are gone forever.

organic

Organic materials were once alive. Compost, made from rotten leaves and vegetables, is organic.

oxygen

Oxygen is a gas in the air that people and animals need to breathe. People and animals breathe in oxygen, while plants release it.

pesticide

A pesticide is made up of chemicals. It is used to kill pests, such as insects, that damage crops.

pollution

Pollution is caused when something harmful or dirty goes into the air, soil, or water. For example, carbon emissions pollute the air.

recycle

To recycle means to break something down and reuse the materials to make something new.

renewable

Things that are renewable can be replaced because they can be made again and will not run out. Solar energy is renewable because energy from the sun will never run out.

rot

Rot means to break down. When organic materials rot, they break down and become part of the soil.

smog

Smog is a type of air pollution. It is caused on hot, sunny days when pollution, such as the exhaust fumes from vehicles, combines with the air to form a thick cloud.

water cycle

The water cycle is the way in which water goes around between the land, the sea, and the air.

Quiz

1 **Which of the following is NOT true?**

a) Plants take in carbon dioxide.
b) Plants give out carbon dioxide.
c) Animals breathe in oxygen.
d) Animals breathe out carbon dioxide.

2 **How much of planet Earth is covered in water?**

a) about a quarter
b) about a third
c) about a half
d) about three-quarters

3 **Put these parts of the water cycle in the correct order:**

a) Water evaporates.
b) Water falls as rain.
c) Water vapor forms clouds.
d) Water collects in lakes and rivers.

4 **Which of the following creates the most pollution?**

a) walking
b) biking
c) driving
d) taking the bus

5 **How many of the following are harmful to wildlife?**

a) litter that's mistaken for food
b) broken glass
c) litter that pollutes a river
d) a plastic bag

6 **How many of the following are renewable materials?**

a) metal
b) plastic
c) wood
d) cotton

7 **How many of the following are organic materials?**

a) banana skin
b) apple core
c) plastic
d) paper

8 **Smog is a mixture of:**

a) smoke and mist
b) smoke and fog
c) smells and mist
d) smells and fog

9 Which of the following can change an animal's habitat?

a) farming
b) buildings
c) roads
d) global warming

10 Which of the following are sources of renewable energy?

a) sun
b) wind
c) water
d) fossil fuels

FURTHER INFORMATION

BOOKS

I'm a Global Citizen: Caring for the Environment by Georgia Amson-Bradshaw, Franklin Watts

World Feature Focus: Habitats by Rebecca Kahn, Franklin Watts

Fact Planet: Pollution by Izzi Howell, Franklin Watts

The Oceans Explored: Ocean Pollution by Claudia Martin, Wayland

WEBSITES

Play games, take quizzes, and watch a video to learn more about climate change: www.brainpop.com/science/earthsystem/climatechange

Learn more about how climate affects the planet: climatekids.nasa.gov

Index